DOMINOES

The First
Flying Man

QUICK STARTER   250 HEADWORDS

T0055096

OXFORD
UNIVERSITY PRESS

Great Clarendon Street, Oxford, OX2 6DP, United Kingdom

Oxford University Press is a department of the University of Oxford.
It furthers the University's objective of excellence in research, scholarship,
and education by publishing worldwide. Oxford is a registered trade
mark of Oxford University Press in the UK and in certain other countries

First published in Dominoes 2012

2020

10 9

ISBN: 978 0 19 424943 0   Book
ISBN: 978 0 19 463900 2   Book and Audio Pack

Printed in China

This book is printed on paper from certified and well-managed sources

ACKNOWLEDGEMENTS

Cover by: Gianluca Garofalo and Matteo Vatani

Illustrations by: Gianluca Garofalo and Matteo Vatani

The publisher would like to thank the following for permission to reproduce photographs: Alamy
Images p.11 (*View of Constantinople, Turkey, 17th century*/The Art Archive); Bridgeman Art
Library Ltd p.25 (*Ascent of the Montgolfier brothers hot-air balloon before the royal family at
Versailles in 1783* (colour engraving), French School, (18th century)/Private Collection);
Corbis pp.3 (Galata Tower, Istanbul/Hemis), 24 (Test Flight of 1902 Wright Glider); Getty
Images p.29 (*Mosque of Sokullu Mehmet Pasha*, by Unknown Artist, 1571–1572/Photoservice
Electa); Oxford University Press p.33 (Istanbul/Photodisc)

DOMINOES

Series Editors: Bill Bowler and Sue Parminter

The First Flying Man

Elspeth Rawstron

Illustrated by Gianluca Garofalo and Matteo Vatani

Elspeth Rawstron studied Drama and English Literature at university and then worked for *The Stage* newspaper in London. She later trained to teach English and moved to Istanbul. She loves books, theatre, art, history, and travel, and she reads a lot in her free time. She can see the Bosphorus and the Galata Tower from her living room window and often wonders about Hezarfen's flight. There is a short account of the flight in a book of travels by the 17th-century Turkish writer Evliya Çelebi.

OXFORD
UNIVERSITY PRESS

Story Characters

Hezarfen Ahmet Çelebi

Mehmet

Ali

Lagari Hasan

The District Chief of Galata

Sultan Murat IV

The Sultan's vizier

Contents

BEFORE READING

1 **This story happens in Istanbul in the 1630s. Which things do you read about in it? What do you think? Tick the boxes.**

a one of the earliest rockets ☐

b a Turkish plane ☐

c Ottoman Sultan Murat IV ☐

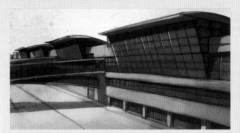

d the Galata Tower ☐

e a Galatasaray footballer ☐

f the airport in Istanbul ☐

2 **Which things happen in the story? What do you think? Tick the boxes.**

a ☐ Hezarfen gets a broken leg when he is learning to fly.

b ☐ Hezarfen meets and talks with Leonardo da Vinci.

c ☐ Hezarfen flies across the Bosphorus.

d ☐ The Sultan is happy and gives money to Hezarfen.

e ☐ The Sultan is afraid and wants to kill Hezarfen.

f ☐ Hezarfen must leave Istanbul in the end.

Chapter 1 – A young man's dream

My story begins in the 1630s. It is the time of the Ottoman **Empire**. **Hezarfen Ahmet Çelebi** is a **clever** young man of those days. He lives in the **district** of Üsküdar, in Istanbul.

Every morning, Hezarfen sits near the Bosphorus **strait**. He looks at the tall **tower** in the district of Galata across the water. The Galata Tower is taller than all the buildings near it.

empire a number of countries that one country controls

Hezarfen Ahmet Çelebi /ˈhezarfen ˌʌhmet ˌtʃelebi/

clever quick-thinking

district part of a big town or city

strait a long thin line of sea water between two pieces of land

tower a very tall thin building

tasty good to eat

ring something round with nothing in the middle

dream to think about something that you want to happen; when you think about something that you want to happen

fly to move through the air

bird an animal that can fly through the sky

'Simit! Would you like a simit?' a man near Hezarfen calls. He has some **tasty** Turkish bread **rings** on his head. But Hezarfen doesn't answer.

Every morning the man cries, 'Would you like a simit?' But Hezarfen never answers.

He doesn't hear or see the man. He is **dreaming**. In his dream, he is **flying** over the Bosphorus with the sea **birds**.

'One day I want to look down from the sky on Istanbul,' he thinks. 'I want to fly across the strait with you birds. But how?'

READING CHECK

These sentences are all false. Correct them.

a The story happens in the 1830s. *(1630s)*

b It is the time of the British Empire.

c Hezarfen is a clever old man.

d The Galata Tower is across the road from his house.

e Every morning, Hezarfen watches the sun in the sky.

f Every night, the simit man comes with some simits.

g Hezarfen always speaks to the man.

h Hezarfen wants to fly over the Galata Tower.

GUESS WHAT

What does Hezarfen do in the next chapter? Tick two boxes.

a He makes one of the earliest planes. ☐

b He looks at some pictures of birds by Leonardo. ☐

c He meets his brother, Lagari Hasan. ☐

d He meets his friends, Mehmet and Ali. ☐

Chapter 2 – Drawings from Italy

Weeks later, Hezarfen is near the Bosphorus again. Again he is looking carefully up at the sea birds in the sky. These days he is making some big **wings** in his **workshop**. He needs some help with the **design**.

'Hezarfen!' someone calls. Hezarfen sees his friend, Mehmet, with a second man. He goes over and says hello to the two of them.

'Hezarfen, this is my brother Ali,' Mehmet says. 'He's got some **drawings** for you from Italy.'

'They're old drawings of birds' wings by Leonardo da Vinci,' Ali says.

'Ah, yes. I know Leonardo's work,' Hezarfen says. 'Let's see them, then.'

Ali gives the drawings to Hezarfen. He looks at them for a minute.

'Interesting,' Hezarfen says. Then he gives them back. 'Thank you, Ali!'

wing a bird flies with two of these

workshop a room where you do work with your hands

design this shows the shape of something in a picture before you make it

drawing a picture

Days later, in Hezarfen's workshop ...

'My wings are ready,' Hezarfen tells his friends.

'Let's see you fly, then,' Mehmet cries.

'Your brother Lagari wants to fly too, I hear,' Ali says. 'Everyone in Istanbul knows that.'

'Yes. Everybody's talking about him these days, I hear. But he isn't interested in wings. He wants to make a **rocket**,' Hezarfen answers.

'So where do you want to **practise**?' Mehmet asks.

'There's a hill not far from here,' Hezarfen says. 'I can practise there.'

rocket a long thin air ship that can fly quickly up into the sky

practise to do something many times so that you can do it well

Hezarfen and Mehmet go up to the **top** of the hill. Ali waits at the foot of it. Mehmet helps Hezarfen with his wings. Then he looks down. 'Hey! Don't **jump** from here,' he says. 'It's **dangerous**.'

'But I must,' Hezarfen says. 'My brother's beginning work on his rocket now. But I want to fly first!' Then he runs and jumps. Mehmet closes his eyes.

top the tallest part of something

jump to move quickly on your feet from one thing to a different thing, or into the air

dangerous that can kill you

READING CHECK

Choose the correct words to complete these sentences.

a Hezarfen is making *little /* *big* wings in his workshop.

b Mehmet is Hezarfen's *brother / friend*.

c Ali is Mehmet's *father / brother*.

d Ali gives pictures by *Michelangelo / Leonardo* to Hezarfen.

e Hezarfen's brother wants to make a *rocket / plane*.

f Hezarfen and his friends go and practise on a *hill / tree*.

g It is *easy / dangerous* to jump from there, Mehmet thinks.

GUESS WHAT

What happens in the next chapter? Tick the boxes.

		Yes	No
a	Hezarfen flies from the hill.	☐	☐
b	He doesn't go very far.	☐	☐
c	He and his friends take the wings to his workshop.	☐	☐
d	Hezarfen must make better wings.	☐	☐
e	He flies up to the sun with his new wings.	☐	☐
f	He falls down into the Bosphorus and nearly dies there.	☐	☐
g	He and his friends go across the Bosphorus to Galata.	☐	☐

Chapter 3 – To Galata

Hezarfen doesn't fly.

He **falls**. Mehmet hears a big **crash** and a cry from the foot of the hill.

He goes quickly down the hill to his friend. Hezarfen is lying under his wings. Ali is next to him.

'His leg's **broken**,' Ali says.

'No, it isn't,' Hezarfen answers. 'My wings are broken. But I'm OK!'

'This time,' Mehmet cries. 'But what about next time? Be careful, my friend. You don't want to die.'

fall to go down quickly

crash a big noise that you make when you hit something and stop suddenly

broken in pieces or not working

They take the broken wings
back to Hezarfen's workshop.

'Now what?' Ali asks.

'I understand more. The design of my wings needs
to be different – bigger and better. But that can wait,'
Hezarfen says. 'Right now I must go and see the
District **Chief** of Galata.'

'Galata!' Mehmet cries. 'Why?'

'I want to fly from the Galata Tower. So I need his
permission for that.'

'Forget it! The district chief never asks people into
his office!' Ali says.

'Let's see,' Hezarfen cries. 'Come on!' And he and his
friends take a **boat** across the Bosphorus.

chief the most
important man in
a place

permission
when you say that
somebody can do
something

boat you go
across water in this

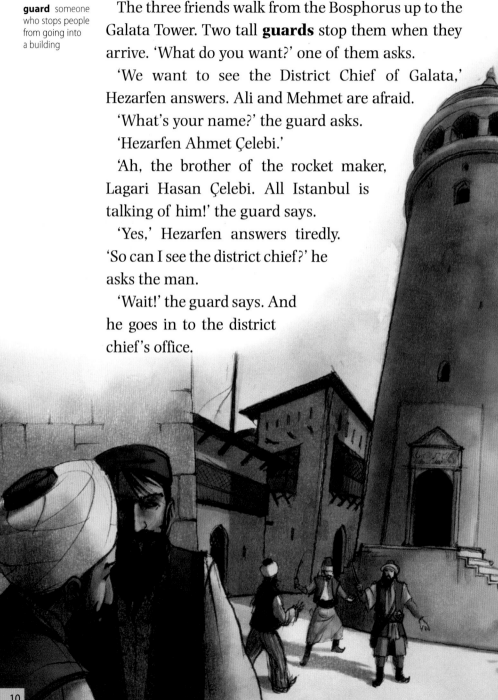

guard someone who stops people from going into a building

The three friends walk from the Bosphorus up to the Galata Tower. Two tall **guards** stop them when they arrive. 'What do you want?' one of them asks.

'We want to see the District Chief of Galata,' Hezarfen answers. Ali and Mehmet are afraid.

'What's your name?' the guard asks.

'Hezarfen Ahmet Çelebi.'

'Ah, the brother of the rocket maker, Lagari Hasan Çelebi. All Istanbul is talking of him!' the guard says.

'Yes,' Hezarfen answers tiredly. 'So can I see the district chief?' he asks the man.

'Wait!' the guard says. And he goes in to the district chief's office.

READING CHECK

Correct nine more mistakes in the story.

falls

Hezarfen ~~flies~~ down from the hill. Mehmet hears a noise and a cry from the foot of the tree. He runs down to his friend, now with Ali. Hezarfen's legs are broken, but he is OK. Hezarfen takes the wings to his workshop without his friends. He must make better wings. Hezarfen wants to fly from the Eiffel Tower. So he and his friends go across the Bosphorus to Üsküdar. Hezarfen wants to speak to the district chief there. Three guards stop them in the street. Ali and Mehmet aren't afraid. Hezarfen gives his name to the guards. One of them knows about Hezarfen's father, Lagari Hasan. Lagari is a bread maker. The guard goes and speaks to the district chief.

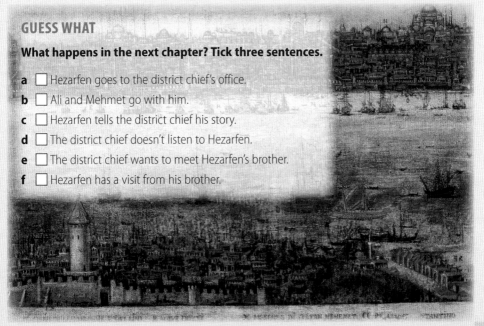

GUESS WHAT

What happens in the next chapter? Tick three sentences.

a ☐ Hezarfen goes to the district chief's office.
b ☐ Ali and Mehmet go with him.
c ☐ Hezarfen tells the district chief his story.
d ☐ The district chief doesn't listen to Hezarfen.
e ☐ The district chief wants to meet Hezarfen's brother.
f ☐ Hezarfen has a visit from his brother.

Chapter 4 — A brother's help

Some time later, the guard takes Hezarfen to the district chief's office. Mehmet and Ali wait at the door.

The district chief listens to Hezarfen's story.

'Very well,' he smiles, 'You can fly from the tower. But be careful. Don't fall and die.'

'No, District Chief,' Hezarfen answers.

'And I'd like to see your brother. Tell him.'

'Yes, District Chief,' Hezarfen says.

'I've got permission,' Hezarfen laughs when he comes out into the street.

'Good!' Ali cries happily.

'What now?' Mehmet asks.

'I must visit Lagari,' Hezarfen says.

So Hezarfen visits his older brother. Lagari is working on his rocket when Hezarfen arrives.

'Nice design,' Hezarfen says.

'Yes,' Lagari answers. 'Perhaps early next year I can fly up into the sky in it. What about you?'

'Me, brother? I want to fly across the sky with my wings later *this* year.'

'So it's a **race**,' Lagari laughs.

'Yes,' Hezarfen smiles. 'But listen. The District Chief of Galata wants to see you.'

'Right. Well, thank you for your visit. Good luck with your wings, Hezarfen!'

'Good luck with your rocket, Lagari!'

And Hezarfen leaves.

race a competition to see who is the fastest

Two weeks later, Hezarfen's new wings are ready.

'Now I can fly from Galata to Üsküdar!' he cries.

'Wait! You must ask the **Sultan**'s permission for that, I think,' Mehmet says. 'And the Sultan says "no" to most people when they ask for things.'

'So what can I do?' Hezarfen cries.

'Listen. These days the District Chief of Galata talks about your brother a lot. Now the Sultan's interested in him, too. Perhaps Lagari can ask the Sultan for a **meeting**,' Ali says.

So Hezarfen goes and speaks to his brother again.

'Yes. I can ask the Sultan,' Lagari smiles. 'But he can always say "no" to a meeting.'

sultan a ruler in some Muslim countries

meeting when people come together to talk about something

READING CHECK

Put the sentences in order. Number them 1–10.

a ☐ Hezarfen finishes his new wings.

b ☐ The district chief listens to Hezarfen's story.

c ☐ Hezarfen tells Mehmet and Ali, 'I've got permission!'

d ☐ Lagari Hasan says, 'I can ask the Sultan for a meeting.'

e ☐ Hezarfen tells Lagari Hasan of the district chief's interest in him.

f ☐ The guard takes Hezarfen to the district chief's office.

g ☐ Hezarfen says, 'Now I can fly from Galata to Üsküdar.'

h ☐ Mehmet says, 'You must ask the Sultan's permission.'

i ☐ Hezarfen speaks to his brother about the Sultan.

j ☐ The district chief tells Hezarfen, 'I'd like to see your brother.'

GUESS WHAT

What happens in the next chapter? Tick one box to finish each sentence.

a Hezarfen is …

   1 ☐ nervous before he meets the Sultan.

   2 ☐ afraid when he speaks to the Sultan.

   3 ☐ happy after he leaves the Sultan.

Hezarfen

b The Sultan …

   1 ☐ kills Hezarfen at once.

   2 ☐ asks Hezarfen for his wings.

   3 ☐ gives his permission to Hezarfen.

The Sultan

c One of the Sultan's viziers …

   1 ☐ wants to help Hezarfen.

   2 ☐ doesn't want to give permission to Hezarfen.

   3 ☐ wants to kill Hezarfen.

The Vizier

Chapter 5 – What does the Sultan say?

So Lagari speaks to the Sultan, and the Sultan says 'yes' to a meeting.

Seven days later, Hezarfen goes to the **palace**. He walks past the Haghia Sophia. He is **nervous**. 'Please give me permission,' he thinks.

Near the Blue **Mosque**, he is more nervous. 'Please say "yes",' he thinks.

Hezarfen stops near the palace. 'The Sultan can of course say, "no". Or, worse – he can say, "Kill that man!"' he thinks.

'I'm Hezarfen Ahmet Çelebi. The Sultan wants to see me,' he tells the palace guard. The man goes in. Hezarfen waits. He is very nervous now.

After an hour, the guard comes back. 'Come with me,' he says to Hezarfen.

Hezarfen **bows** very nervously when he meets the Sultan. '**Your Highness**, I want to fly across the Bosphorus,' he says. The Sultan smiles.

'Ah, yes. You're Lagari Hasan's brother,' he says.

'Yes, Your Highness,' Hezarfen answers. Then he asks for the Sultan's permission.

'You have it,' the Sultan says. 'You must fly across the Bosphorus tomorrow.'

'With a good wind,' Hezarfen says. 'But without it – what then, Your Highness?'

'You must ask God for a wind,' the Sultan smiles.

'Your Highness,' a **vizier** says quietly. 'People can walk with their legs. But we don't have wings. Is a flying man good in God's eyes?'

palace a big house where a sultan lives

nervous a little afraid

mosque Muslims go here to pray

bow to put your head down when you meet somebody important

Your Highness you say this when you talk to a sultan

wind air that moves

vizier an important man in the Muslim world; he helps a sultan

'Listen,' the Sultan answers. 'We can think of new things with our **brains**. And our brains come from God. The first flying man must be an Ottoman, I say.'

'Yes, Your Highness,' the vizier says. But he looks angrily at Hezarfen.

That evening, Hezarfen is not happy.

'There's no wind!' he tells Mehmet and Ali.

brain this is in your head and you think with it

READING CHECK

Are these sentences true or false?

		True	False
a	The Sultan says 'yes' to a meeting with Hezarfen.	☑	☐
b	Before his meeting with the Sultan, Hezarfen is nervous.	☐	☐
c	Hezarfen tells the Sultan, 'I want to fly over the Haghia Sophia.'	☐	☐
d	He asks for the Sultan's permission.	☐	☐
e	The Sultan gives his permission to Hezarfen.	☐	☐
f	The Sultan tells Hezarfen, 'You must fly next week.'	☐	☐
g	One of the Sultan's viziers is not happy about this.	☐	☐
h	'Is a flying boat good in God's eyes?' he asks.	☐	☐
i	'The first flying man must be an Englishman,' says the Sultan.	☐	☐
j	Hezarfen is very happy that night because there is no wind.	☐	☐

GUESS WHAT

What happens in the next chapter? Circle the words to complete the sentences.

a There is *no* / *lots of* wind the next day.

b Hezarfen *falls* / *jumps* from the Galata Tower.

c He *flies across the Bosphorus* / *dies in a Galata street*.

d The Sultan gives *money* / *a palace* to Hezarfen.

e Hezarfen *stays in Istanbul* / *leaves for Algeria* in the end.

Chapter 6 – Hezarfen's reward

The next morning, there is lots of wind. Hezarfen stands happily with his wings at the top of the Galata Tower. Suddenly, he jumps. 'He's falling!' people cry. But he is not falling. He is flying with his big white wings over the houses of Galata.

Hezarfen's friends Mehmet and Ali run with the people down the streets to the Bosphorus. Hezarfen flies out over the water.

land to come down to the ground, or into the sea

'I'm flying,' he cries. 'People can fly!' He **lands** across the strait in Üsküdar, a happy man.

The next day, the Sultan has a meeting with his viziers at the palace. 'People can fly,' he cries excitedly. 'And the first flying man is an Ottoman. That's good for our Empire. Hezarfen needs a **reward**.'

'But, Your Highness,' the vizier nearest to him says. 'Flying men can land in our palaces and kill us. They're dangerous.'

The Sultan thinks about this. 'Hmmm. Yes, I see. Perhaps you're right. So what must we do with Hezarfen then?' he asks.

'Kill him,' the vizier answers.

reward a thing that people give or do to somebody after they do something good

exile to make
somebody leave
their home country
or town after they
do something that
you don't like

gold expensive
yellow metal

coin metal
money

'I can't do that,' the Sultan cries.

'Then **exile** him,' the vizier says.

So the Sultan calls Hezarfen Ahmet Çelebi to the palace. He gives a reward of a thousand **gold coins** to him. Then he exiles him to Algeria.

Hezarfen says goodbye to his brother and his friends. He leaves Istanbul that evening.

After that, he can fly over the Bosphorus with the birds in his dreams. But he can never go back to Istanbul again.

'And what about Lagari and his rocket?' you ask.

Well, perhaps one day I can tell you that story, too.

READING CHECK

Choose the correct pictures.

a Which building does Hezarfen jump from?

1 ☐ the Haghia Sophia   2 ☑ the Galata Tower

b Where do Mehmet and Ali run?

1 ☐ to the Bosphorus   2 ☐ to the Blue Mosque

c Which Istanbul district does Hezarfen land in?

1 ☐ Galata   2 ☐ Üsküdar

d What does the Sultan want to do to Hezarfen?

1 ☐ give money to him   2 ☐ kill him

e What does Hezarfen do in the end?

1 ☐ stays in Istanbul   2 ☐ leaves Istanbul

GUESS WHAT
What happens to Lagari Hasan? Tick the boxes and add your own ideas.

a ☐ He never finishes his rocket.

b ☐ He finishes his rocket.

c ☐ He flies up into the sky when the Sultan has his first daughter.

d ☐ He falls from his rocket and dies.

e ☐ He lands in the sea and is OK.

f ☐ The Sultan gives money to him.

g ☐ He goes and lives in Galata in the end.

h ☐ ....

i ☐ ....

PROJECTS

Project A *Famous flyers of the past*

1 Read the text about the Wright brothers and complete the table.

The Wright brothers Wilbur – (1867–1912) and Orville (1871–1948) – are famous American flyers. Many people know their names today because of their flights near the town of Kitty Hawk in a plane with an engine on December 17th 1903 – a first in the history of flying. These days you can visit the Wright Brothers National Memorial in North Carolina, USA and see models of their old planes.

Names and dates of flyers	
Nationality	
Famous for which 'flying first'	
Place of this 'flying first'	
Date of this 'flying first'	
Things to do these days connected with the brothers	

2 **Read the notes in the table about the Montgolfier Brothers and complete the text about them.**

Names and dates of flyers	Joseph Montgolfier (1740-1810) and Etienne Montgolfier (1745-1799)
Nationality	French
Famous for which 'flying first'	their flight of a hot-air balloon in front of lots of people
Place of this 'flying first'	in the town of Annonay
Date of this 'flying first'	4 June 1783
Things to do these days connected with the brothers	See a model of one of the Montgolfier brothers' balloons at the Science Museum in London

The . . . . brothers – . . . .
(. . . . . – . . . .) and . . . .
. . . . (1745–1799) – are
famous . . . . flyers. Many
people know their names today because of
their . . . .
. . . .
– . . . . in front of
lots of people in . . . .
. . . .
on . . . .
. . . . – a first in the history of flying.
These days you can visit the . . . .
. . . . in . . . . and see a
. . . . of one of their . . . .

3 **Find out more about a famous flyer and write a short text about him or her.**

Ibn Firnas   SABIHA GÖKÇEN   Amelia Earhart

Amy Johnson   Valentina Tereshkova   Yuri Gagarin

Project B *Writing about your dream*

1 Read this dream text. Which character in *The First Flying Man* is it about?

> I make my money selling things in the street.
> I want to buy a bread shop with this money.
> I want to make the best bread in Istanbul.
> My dream is to be the Sultan's favourite baker.
> My dream is to bake all the bread and cakes in his palace.

2 These two dream texts are mixed together. Letter each line G (Guard) or B (Boatman).

a .... I work at the Sultan's palace.

b .... I take people across the Bosphorus.

c .... I want to sell my old boat and buy a big boat.

d .... I want to go away across the sea.

e .... I want to do more than stand at the door.

f .... I want to stand always near the Sultan.

g .... My dream is to visit many far away countries.

h .... My dream is to speak quietly in his ear.

i .... My dream is to be one of the Sultan's viziers.

j .... My dream is to see all of the Ottoman Empire.

The Guard

The Boatman

3 Choose a new story character. Write a dream text about them. Your classmates must read it, and guess the character.

I..
I want to ....
I want to ....
My dream is to ....
My dream is to ....

4 What important thing do you want to do in your life? Write a dream text for you. Read it aloud to your classmates.

....
....
....
....
....

WORD WORK 1

1 Find words in the feathers to match the pictures.

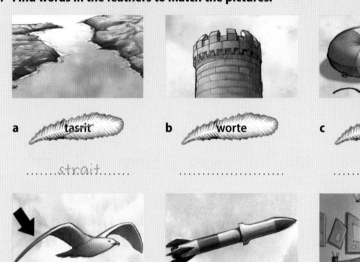

a tasrit

b worte

c gnri

........strait.......

....

....

d gniw

e toreck

f krowhops

....

....

....

2 Complete the sentences with words from Chapters 1 and 2.

a I like this..drawing...by Leonardo. It's a.................for a bicycle.

b In the 1630s, the Ottoman.................is very big.

c She can't read or write. She isn't very................. .

d Which.................of London do you live in?

e Some birds can run, but they can't................. .

f Do you often.................at night?

g When you.................a lot, you learn to do things better.

h Mmm! This apple is very................. .

i Do you want to walk to the.................of the hill?

j Can you.................from this tree to that tree?

k Don't play in the street. It's................. .

WORD WORK 2

1 Find nine more words from Chapters 3 and 4 in the letter square.

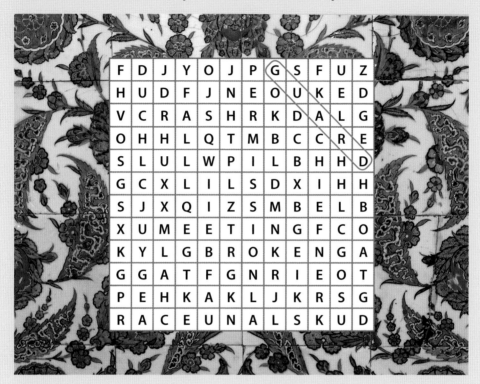

F	D	J	Y	O	J	P	G	S	F	U	Z
H	U	D	F	J	N	E	O	U	K	E	D
V	C	R	A	S	H	R	K	D	A	L	G
O	H	H	L	Q	T	M	B	C	C	R	E
S	L	U	L	W	P	I	L	B	H	H	D
G	C	X	L	I	L	S	D	X	I	H	H
S	J	X	Q	I	Z	S	M	B	E	L	B
X	U	M	E	E	T	I	N	G	F	C	O
K	Y	L	G	B	R	O	K	E	N	G	A
G	G	A	T	F	G	N	R	I	E	O	T
P	E	H	K	A	K	L	J	K	R	S	G
R	A	C	E	U	N	A	L	S	K	U	D

2 Complete each sentence with one of the words from Activity 1.

a 'Where's the .... *guard* .... ?' 'He's over there, near the door.'

b I can't tell the time because my watch is . . . .

c Please don't get out of the tower window. You can . . . . and die easily.

d Ask your mother for her . . . . before you say 'yes'.

e 'Who is the . . . . ?' the visitor asks some villagers.

f When the car hits the tree, there's a big . . . .

g Which is the fastest bicycle? Let's have a . . . . and see.

h Murat IV is the . . . . in the story.

i We can talk about this at the office . . . . later.

j 'How can we go across the Bosphorus?' 'Let's take a . . . . !'

WORD WORK 3

1 These words don't match the pictures. Correct them.

a ~~mosque~~

........palace........

b gold

....

c wind

....

d coin

....

e brain

....

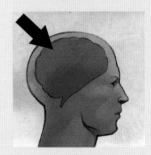

f palace

....

2 Complete the sentences with words from Chapters 5 and 6 in the correct form.

a Everyone b o w s in front of the Sultan when they meet him.

b Monday's my first day at work and I'm _ _ _ _ _ _ _ about it.

c You must call the Sultan '_ _ _ _   _ _ _ _ _ _ _ _'.

d When the Sultan's _ _ _ _ _ _ speaks, the Sultan listens carefully to him.

e Her mother gives a _ _ _ _ _ _ to her when she helps a lot in the house.

f His plane _ _ _ _ _ at Glasgow airport at ten o'clock tonight.

g Why does the Sultan _ _ _ _ _ Hezarfen from Istanbul?

GRAMMAR

GRAMMAR CHECK

Possessive adjectives

We use possessive adjectives to say who something or someone belongs to.

Murat IV is their Sultan. (= the Ottomans')

Lagari is his brother. (= Hezarfen's)

Rawstron is her family name. (= the author of the story, Elspeth's)

1 **Replace the underlined words in these phrases with the possessive adjectives in the box.**

> her   his   its   my   our   ~~their~~   their   your

a <u>Mehmet and Ali's</u> home ..... their ...... home

b <u>the Sultan's</u> palace .... palace

c '<u>Hezarfen and Lagari's</u> dream,' Hezarfen and Lagari say. '.................. dream'

d '<u>Hezarfen's</u> reward,' the Sultan tells Hezarfen. '.................. reward'

e '<u>The Sultan's</u> young brother,' the Sultan says. '.................. young brother'

f '<u>Mother's</u> room,' the Sultan says. '.................. room'

g <u>the brothers'</u> workshops .... workshops

h <u>the bird's</u> head .... head

2 **Complete the sentences with the correct possessive adjectives.**

a Mehmet and Ali say, 'Hezarfen is ...... our .... friend.'

b Hezarfen looks at the drawing of the dead bird and .... wing.

c 'I'm OK! .... arms and legs aren't broken,' Hezarfen says.

d Mehmet and Ali are afraid of the guards and .... angry faces.

e 'What's .... name?' one of the guards asks Hezarfen.

f 'We can think of new things with .... brains,' the Sultan says.

g In the end, Hezarfen is not happy because the reward for all .... work is exile.

h Elspeth can see the Bosphorus from .... window.

GRAMMAR CHECK

Prepositions of place and time

Prepositions of place tell you **where** something happens. Prepositions of time tell you **when** something happens. Look at the table.

	at	**in**	**on**
Place	the door	Galata	a hill
	the top	Istanbul	the Bosphorus
Time	night	the 1630s	a night with no wind
	12 o'clock	the evening	Friday

3 Mark the phrases P (place) or T (time).

a at the front ......P......
b in October ....
c on New Year's Day ....

d on the sea ....
e in Italy ....
f at the weekend ....

4 Circle *at*, *on*, or *in*.

a (on)/ *at* / *in* 1st January
b *on* / *at* / *in* the sky
c *on* / *at* / *in* midnight
d *on* / *at* / *in* the afternoon

e *on* / *at* / *in* a nice district
f *on* / *at* / *in* a day with wind
g *on* / *at* / *in* Üsküdar
h *on* / *at* / *in* the foot of a hill

5 Complete the sentences with *at*, *on*, or *in*.

a The guards stop Hezarfen and his friends ......*in*...... the street.
b Hezarfen meets the district chief .... a good time.
c Mehmet and Ali see the wings .... Hezarfen's workshop.
d Hezarfen is nervous .... the day of his meeting with the Sultan.
e Herzafen stands .... the tower window and looks down.
f He flies across to Üsküdar .... the morning.
g There are lots of boats .... the Bosphorus.
h Hezarfen dies .... 1640 .... Algeria.

GRAMMAR CHECK

Articles: a/an, the

We use a/an when we talk about a singular noun and it is not clear which of many things we mean. We use a before a word beginning with a consonant sound, and an before a word beginning with a vowel sound.

There is a man near Hezarfen.   *It's an interesting story.*

We use the when we talk about singular and plural nouns and it is clear which of many things we mean.

The man cries, 'Simit!'   *Some people know the story.*

6 Complete the sentences with *a/an* or *the*.

a The Galata Tower stands on a hill in . . .the. . Galata district of Istanbul.

b Hezarfen has . . . . old workshop not far from his house. He makes interesting new things in . . . . workshop.

c Istanbul is on . . . . strait and near . . . . sea, too. . . . . name of . . . . strait in Istanbul is . . . . Bosphorus.

d Hezarfen has . . . . interesting dream. He wants to fly through . . . . sky.

e Hezarfen looks up carefully at . . . . birds over his head. Perhaps he can learn something from . . . . design of their wings.

f . . . . vizier is standing next to Sultan Murat IV. . . . . vizier says some bad things about Hezarfen.

g The Sultan gives . . . . reward to Hezarfen soon after he flies across the strait. Some of . . . . reward is good – . . . . money. But some of it is bad – . . . . exile to Algeria.

║ DOMINOES Your Choice ║

Read *Dominoes* for pleasure, or to develop language skills. It's your choice.

Each *Domino* reader includes:
- a good story to enjoy
- integrated activities to develop reading skills and increase vocabulary
- task-based projects – perfect for CEFR portfolios
- contextualized grammar activities

Each *Domino* pack contains a reader, and an excitingly dramatized audio recording of the story

If you liked this *Domino*, read these:

Ali Baba and the Forty Thieves
Retold by Janet Hardy-Gould
Ali Baba finds a thieves' treasure cave and he is suddenly rich. Then his brother Kasim visits the cave, and things go wrong. The forty thieves find Kasim there, kill him, and cut his body into four pieces. What can Ali Baba do? He wants to bury his brother quietly, but how can he? Morgiana, his servant-girl, has the answer. But what can she do when the thieves find Ali Baba and want to kill him, too?

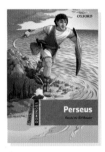

Perseus
Retold by Bill Bowler
Perseus is the son of Danae, Princess of Argos, and the god Zeus. When he is very young, his mother moves with him to live on the island of Seriphos.
Later, Polydectes – the king of Seriphos – wants to marry Danae. Perseus says 'no' to this, so Polydectes sends the young man away for the head of Medusa. Medusa is a she-monster, with snakes for hair. Can Perseus find and kill Medusa? And what happens after he goes back to Seriphos?

	CEFR	Cambridge Exams	IELTS	TOEFL iBT	TOEIC
Level 3	B1	PET	4.0	57-86	550
Level 2	A2–B1	KET-PET	3.0-4.0	–	390
Level 1	A1–A2	YLE Flyers/KET	3.0	–	225
Starter & Quick Starter	A1	YLE Movers	1.0–2.0	–	–

You can find details and a full list of books and teachers' resources on our website:
www.oup.com/elt/gradedreaders